Even now, says th._____._____h
fasting, and weeping, and mourning. (Joel 2:12)

A cartoon in The Wall Street Journal shows a prophet carrying a sign which reads: "Repent...(if you have already repented, disregard this notice)."

Reflection

Oh no, it's that time again: Lent. Few of us are comfortable in committing to change (ask yourself how well you have done with your New Year's resolutions), sacrifice, and penance. As much as we may find it uncomfortable, deep within we know it is beneficial and needed. We just wish there was an easier way. It's a lot like the man who went to the doctor, who took x-rays that showed some problems. The operation suggested by the doctor would be very painful and very expensive. The doctor pointed out, however, that for much less money he could just touch up the x-rays.

Real change takes a firm commitment. Forty days may frighten us. At times it can seem like forever. Besides, how can we change something that we have been doing for so many years? The key is simply to take one step at a time, one day at a time. And knowing that the Lord is with us every step of the way takes the pressure off.

Daily Prayer

Dear Lord, today I begin Lent. I am not always excited about Lent; in fact, I often dread it. It seems so long and burdensome. Help me realize, Lord, that it is not so much what I do, but why I do it. I want to be more like you; I want to be your light in the world. O Lord, please walk with me today. Amen.

Thursday after
Ash Wednesday

Today I have set before you life and prosperity, death and doom.
(Deuteronomy 30:15)

At a party, the hostess served a guest a sip of punch and told him it was spiked. Next, she served some to a minister. "I would rather commit adultery than allow liquor to pass through my lips!" he shouted.

Hearing this, the first man poured his punch back and shouted, "Hey, I didn't know we had a choice!"

Reflection

Choices—every day we make them, some good, some bad, and many indifferent. Today we have so many options and choices, from hundreds of channels on TV to the thousands of movies at the video store. Lent may be a good time to examine our choices: our friends, music, entertainment, prayer time, and the like. The list is endless. What are our priorities? What are the goals we have set for ourselves? Are our choices helping us accomplish these? Life, not false pleasure and hope, is only found in Christ.

Daily Prayer

Lord, I feel empty inside. I know something is missing, but I don't know what it is. So many "things" promise me happiness and fulfillment. I hear about and see them advertised in magazines, on TV, and on billboards. They certainly look appealing. Yet I know deep down that my peace and true joy is found in you. Help me, Lord, not to be fooled or swayed but to keep my life centered on you. Amen.

REPENT, IT'S LENT

Daily Stories, Prayers, and Reflections

REV. THOMAS CONNERY

My Dear Friend in Jesus,

Lent is once again upon us. This may cause different reactions in different people: eagerness about the chance to grow in our spiritual life, disdain for the sacrifices Lent demands, or just plain indifference to it all.

But Lent is a tremendous gift to us, an opportunity to grow our faith and in our love for God. It is a time to get to know ourselves and the Lord just a little bit better, a time to prepare for celebrating the holy season of Easter.

Realize that as we journey through Lent we are not alone. We are united with all Christians throughout the world. This is a unique time for blessing and growth.

Know that a religion that does nothing, costs nothing, suffers nothing—is worth nothing. May our faith be our most prized gift and may it be renewed this lenten season.

Your friend,

Father Tom Connery

Acknowledgment

My sincere appreciation and thanks to Helen Smorto for her insight, assistance, and skill in completing this book.

Friday after Ash Wednesday

Shout out, do not hold back!...Tell my people their wickedness, and the house of Jacob their sins.

(Isaiah 58:1)

In a "Charlie Brown" cartoon, little Linus, looking very forlorn, asks Lucy, "Why are you always so anxious to criticize me?" Lucy, looking very self-righteous, replies, "I just think I have a knack for seeing other people's faults." Linus turns indignant. "What about your *own* faults?" he asks. "I have a knack for overlooking them," answers Lucy.

Reflection

Most of us are like Lucy. We have a knack for overlooking our own faults but easily find them in others. Yet it is beneficial to know our weaknesses, and a good friend can help us in this area. We may not like to hear what our friends have to say, but listening to them is a monumental step in the right direction.

Maybe this Lent is the time to take a good hard look at ourselves. It is not easy but it can lead to great growth. May the Lord give us the courage to grow·and the grace to listen.

Daily Prayer

Lord, how often I look in the mirror and fail to see the real me. I get so absorbed in the externals that I am blind to what really counts. This Lent, Lord, I want to see myself as I really am. Help me to see not with eyes of judgment but with eyes of caring acceptance and, when necessary, gentle prodding. Help me to deal honestly and sincerely with what I may not like in myself. Amen.

Saturday after Ash Wednesday

The healthy do not need a doctor; sick people do. I have not come to invite the self-righteous to a change of heart, but sinners.

(Luke 5:31–32)

There is a beautiful legend in which someone has pictured the Day of the Lord, the Last Day. Up in Paradise everyone is celebrating, dancing, singing, and shouting with great jubilation. Everyone except Jesus. Jesus is standing very quietly in the shadows of the gates of Paradise. Someone asks him what he is doing in the midst of all this celebration. In a gentle voice Jesus says, "I am waiting for Judas." God's forgiving love!

Reflection

The danger of Lent is to focus on how much we are doing: prayers offered, Masses attended, or pleasures given up. The truth is, it is always Jesus who initiates, seeks, and longs for us. The greatest step we can take this Lent is to accept wholeheartedly God's healing and redeeming love. Today surrender to God's all-embracing love and live as a person loved by God.

Daily Prayer

O Lord, my Redeemer, I am saved by your grace. How fortunate I am that you love me so much! I need not be perfect for you to accept me as I am. When I fall, you are there to pick me up. When I falter, you strengthen me, and when I fail, you forgive me. I praise and thank you for your compassionate love, and may I forgive others as you have forgiven me. Amen.

First Sunday of Lent

Everyone who calls on the name of the Lord will be saved.

(Romans 10:13)

To find out exactly what goes through the mind of a person falling into space, a group of aerodynamic scientists hired a young man who had never parachuted before. They trained and equipped him, wired him for sound, and instructed him to record in full detail all his thoughts and sensations as he fell. To their dismay when the tapes were played back all that could be heard the entire way down was an exuberant "Whee-ee-ee!"

Reflection

What did the scientists expect? It sounds too simple. They were expecting some elaborate, complicated, highly rationalized response and all they heard was: Whee-ee-ee!

Our own salvation can seem too easy, too simple. So much so that we attempt to complicate it and confuse it. The core of our faith is believing in the Lord Jesus, that in him we are redeemed. Once you truly believe in Jesus' saving power, everything else falls into place. Perhaps you can offer a simple prayer of praise by reciting over and over the name of our savior, Jesus!

Daily Prayer

Dear Father, can it really be that simple? Am I saved by just calling on the name of your son, Jesus? Father, I want to call on his name not just with my lips but with every fiber of my being. I want to have the conviction, the confidence, that when I call on him, he is present. Through your Holy Spirit, strengthen my faith. I ask this in the name of Jesus, your son. Amen.

Monday the First Week

I assure you, as often as you did it for one of my least brothers or sisters, you did it for me. (Matthew 25:40)

Alfred Adler, a famous psychologist, once put an ad in the paper for his Fourteen-Day Cure Plan. He claimed that he could cure anyone of any mental or emotional difficulty in just fourteen days if they would do exactly what he told them to.

One day a woman who was extremely lonely came to see Adler. He told her he could cure her of her loneliness in just fourteen days if she would follow his advice. She was not very enthusiastic, but still she asked, "What do you want me to do?"

Adler replied, "If you will do something for someone else every day for fourteen days, at the end of that time your loneliness will be gone." She objected profusely, "Why should I do anything for anybody else? No one ever does anything for me." Adler supposedly responded, "Well, then maybe it will take you twenty-one days."

Reflection

Whether it takes us fourteen days, twenty-one days, or a whole lifetime, our goal should be to serve others. Not only is it a cure for loneliness, but it is our way of serving Christ. This Lent let us each choose one way we can serve Christ by ministering to the least of God's people.

Daily Prayer

Dear Lord, you make it so easy to serve you, but at the same time, so challenging. To find you, I must seek you in those I prefer to ignore. You are the beggar, the homeless, the addict, the old, and the young. If I wish to love you, I must love those I find hard to love. Help me this Lent to do something to give of myself to someone I would normally walk by. Help me to see your face in them. Amen.

Tuesday the First Week

So shall my word be that goes forth from my mouth; It shall not return to me void, but shall do my will, achieving the end for which I sent it. (Isaiah 55:11)

The reporter was interviewing the local centenarian. "The secret of a long life, as I see it," the old fellow explained, "is to make sure you keep waking up morning after morning."

"And what is your formula for accomplishing that, sir?" asked the reporter.

"Well," the aged one drawled, "living a clean life helps. But the most important thing is to drink lots of water before retiring at night. Then you'll *have* to wake up the next morning."

Reflection

A sure plan for us Christians is to follow God's Word. It never fails. Sure, at times it may seem that God has turned a deaf ear to us, that we are merely spinning our wheels, that nothing makes a difference. But God promises to fulfill his Word—always! Today, trust in God. Believe in his Word, even if it seems hopeless. God's Word shall not return void. Believe it!

Daily Prayer

Heavenly Father, there are so many options, choices, and opinions. I get confused and puzzled. I once knew what was right and wrong, but now I am not so sure! It is a comfort and a blessing to know that your commands are timeless, your Word remains true. Help me not to falter or doubt, but to be confident and strong. May I do your will and achieve what you have created me to do. Amen.

Wednesday the First Week

When God saw by their actions how they turned from their evil ways, he repented of the evil that he had threatened to do to them.

(Jonah 3:10)

❧

The great novelist had gone mad, but now there seemed some hope for his recovery. For six months, he had been sitting at his typewriter pounding out a novel. Finally, he pronounced it completed and brought the book to his psychiatrist, who eagerly began reading it aloud:

"General Jackson leaped upon his faithful horse and yelled, 'Giddyap, giddyap, giddyap, giddyap...'" The doctor thumbed through the rest of the manuscript. "There's nothing here but 500 pages of giddyaps!" he exclaimed.

"Stubborn horse," explained the writer.

Reflection

Fortunately, the people of Nineveh were not quite that stubborn. Many heard Jonah's warning of doom, repented, and turned to the Lord. At times we can be stubborn and delay in heeding God's request. These forty days of Lent are our time to surrender to the Lord, to change our ways and live as children of God. With God's grace, may this be so. Why not start today?

Daily Prayer

Lord, I know I should change my ways. I want to change, but I always manage to put it off. I am too busy, too tired, or too lazy to expend the effort. Besides, though I may not be perfect, I am comfortable with who I am. Yet I know this is merely a cop-out, a poor excuse. Maybe this Lent I can get started. Help me, Lord, to make that change. Amen.

Thursday the First Week

Treat others the way you would have them treat you: this sums up the law and the prophets. (Matthew 7:12)

There is a story about an old missionary out in the field who needed an assistant. They sent him a young scholar with a Ph.D. in theology. When he arrived the young man had to speak to the natives through the old man because he didn't know the language. In his first talk to these simple but wonderful people, the young man delved deep into his learning and said, "Truth is absolute and relative. The gospel is absolute truth, but its application is relative to immediate needs." Then he paused for a moment for the old missionary to translate this. The old missionary scratched his head and with a puzzled look across his face, arose and simply stated, "He said that he's awfully glad to be with you."

Reflection

When you get right down to it, the gospel is really quite simple. Oh, we may try to enhance it, analyze it, and complicate it, but it is really quite basic: "Treat others the way you want to be treated." So simple and yet so difficult. This Lent, let us examine how we speak to others and how we treat members of our family, our coworkers, our friends. Let us be as considerate of others as we wish them to be toward us.

Daily Prayer

Dear God, I know how I expect and want to be treated. Yet I often forget that others wish the same from me. Help me, Lord, to be understanding, patient, and sensitive to others' needs.

Even when I am rushed or tired, let me not hurry by, or behave rudely and inconsiderately to others. Remind me, Lord, to always treat others as I wish to be treated. This not only pleases them but it pleases you. Amen.

Friday the First Week

If the wicked turn away from all their sins and do what is right and just, they shall surely live. (Ezekiel 18:21)

A man opened up the morning paper and was shocked to find his name mistakenly printed in the obituary column. Greatly disturbed he went to the newspaper office and complained to the editor: "This is terrible! Your error will cause me no end of embarrassment and may even mean a loss of business. How could you do such a thing?"

The editor expressed regrets but the man remained angry and unreasonable. Finally the editor said in disgust: "Cheer up, fellow, I'll put your name in the birth column tomorrow and give you a fresh start!"

Reflection

When we confess our sins, it is like receiving a fresh start. No matter how often we fail, if we sincerely seek forgiveness, God promises to forgive. Always! Lent is an excellent time to make a fresh start, to begin again, and to ask God's forgiveness for our sins. What's holding us back?

Daily Prayer

Heavenly Father, you are the greatest. Who can always forgive and never stop forgiving as you eternally do? Your abundant love astounds me. I am ashamed and embarrassed by my sins and maybe too proud to ask for forgiveness. How foolish I am. May I take advantage of your loving mercy, confess my sins, and live as a newborn child in your sight. Amen.

Saturday the First Week

Today you are making this agreement with the Lord: he is to be your God and you are to walk in his ways. (Deuteronomy 26:17)

※

During the earthquake in Los Angeles back in 1994, you might have heard of the fortuitous luck of some people who happened not to be in bed at the time of the quake. In Encino, for example, a young man who was house-sitting fell asleep watching TV in the living room. The earthquake flipped him off the couch like a penny. Shaken but unhurt, he searched the house and one of the first things he noticed was that the doors to the bedroom closet had been knocked off their tracks and landed on the pillow. If he had been sleeping there, he would have been crushed to death.

Reflection
This young man in California felt quite fortunate, which indeed he was. We are all under God's care and protection, even if it may not be as dramatic as that. When we encounter struggles and difficulties, we can't give in to discouragement or despair. We have to remember that we belong to God and God will care for us. Be at peace. Our Father knows best.

Daily Prayer
Lord, why am I so troubled and anxious? Why do I let my cares and concerns rob me of my peace and security? I forget that I belong to you. I begin to think that I am in control, that I must handle my struggles alone. How foolish I am. I have you, O Lord, with me; what more could I seek? Lord, let me allow you to be my God, and I will be your child. That's all I need to do. Amen.

Second Sunday of Lent

Be imitators of me, my brothers and sisters, and do not live as enemies of the cross of Christ. (Philippians 3:17–18)

A cab driver in Mexico had quite an eventful day recently. In the morning he helped a woman give birth in his car; in the afternoon he saved a man from choking to death; and he topped off the evening by breaking up a robbery. He's just lucky he's not a cab driver in New York where that's considered a slow day.

Reflection

Our days pale in comparison to that cab driver's day. Most of them are routine: get up, go to work, care for the kids, go to bed, and begin again the next morning. This sometimes seems boring and leaves us restless. Though we cannot imitate the cab driver, we *can* imitate St. Paul. How? We imitate Paul in following Christ and by our patience, forgiveness, and willingness to serve. This also means dying to ourselves every day, which is not easy or as courageous as breaking up a robbery. But we do what we are able to do. In Lent may we have the courage to imitate St. Paul's Christian behavior.

Daily Prayer

Dear God, there are so many images, models, and false hopes in the world. We worry about our children mimicking poor role models. We fear getting caught up in the pressures to follow the ways of the world. Yet as your followers, we must choose what is right and imitate the saints who reflected Christ for us. We may not be in the headlines or on the evening news, but help us realize that when we follow you we are choosing the better prize. Amen.

Monday the Second Week

We have sinned, been wicked and done evil; we have rebelled and departed from your commandments and your laws. (Daniel 9:5)

Newspaper columnist John Sinor tells of the time he was sent by the city editor to rescue a cat stuck in a tree: "The photographer and I got a long ladder. When we put it up against the tree, however, the cat came down by itself. There was only one thing to do. Catch the cat and take it back up the tree so that we could get a picture of me taking it down. We ran the picture the next day of me taking the cat down. There was only one problem: the rival paper in town ran a picture of me putting the cat up."

Reflection
The beauty of today's first reading from the Book of Daniel is the honesty of the Israelites. No games, no alibis, no excuses: they admit that they have turned away from God. I have heard that in counseling therapy a significant turning point arrives when the client is able to grasp this paradox: when we accept our limitations, the chance for personal growth and development is limitless. As long as we spend our energy and time in denial, we can't grow. The first step in self-transformation is to admit the need for change. May we be as honest as the Israelites in this regard.

Daily Prayer
Compassionate God, Lent is a time for change, for owning up to our mistakes, and for being honest in our shortcomings. Yet I try to avoid change as much as possible. I compare myself to others and believe that I am not as bad as they. I find excuses or reasons to blame someone else or circumstances for my failures. Lord, help me realize that I need to face the truth. Help me not to play games anymore but to face myself honestly. Amen.

Tuesday the Second Week

Cease doing evil and learn to do good. (Isaiah 1:16–17)

An employee was passing his boss' office when he heard an angry yell. Ducking his head inside, he saw that his boss was glaring at an envelope. When the amused employee inquired what was wrong, the boss answered, "Never lick an envelope after eating Oreos!"

Reflection

A simple lesson and a practical one at that. Isaiah, too, offers us a swift word of wisdom. How do I become holy, more Godlike, more the person that God wants me to be? Simply "cease doing evil and learn to do good."

This advice sounds quite easy, and it is if we follow it. But often, we don't. Are our choices made for the good, according to what God wants? Or are they better left undone? Are we truly following God's plan for us? During this time of renewal, may we open our minds and hearts in learning to do good and avoid evil.

Daily Prayer

O Lord, I often complicate my life. I think that I know what is right for me and I go my own way. I get swayed by false promises, a life-style pictured in commercials that doesn't exist. I allow my selfish desires to drown your word of truth. I am even foolish enough to believe that I can find happiness without you. Help me to put into practice the wisdom of avoiding evil and doing good, today and every day. Let me begin now. Amen.

Wednesday the Second Week

Anyone among you who aspires to greatness must serve the rest, and whoever wants to rank first among you, must serve the needs of all.
                                                        (Matthew 20:26–27)

An eighty-five-year-old woman was being interviewed on her birthday. What advice would she have for people her age, the reporter asked. "Well," said the old dear, "at our age it is very important to keep using all our potential or it dries up. It is important to be with people and if at all possible, to earn one's living through service. That's what keeps us alive and well."

"May I ask what exactly you do for a living at your age?"

"I look after an old lady in my neighborhood," was her unexpected, delightful reply.

Reflection

We are never too young or too old to be servants to each other. Helping others not only keeps us physically young, but spiritually alive as well. The core of the Christian life-style is our service to each other. This Lent may be the appropriate time to ask ourselves how and to whom we are of service. There are many possibilities: the homebound, the ill, children, or even someone in our own family. What is most important is not who we serve, but that we are a servant to someone.

Daily Prayer

Dear God, I am often fooled by the world's values. I think that if I dress a certain way, drive a particular car, or have a fancy title before my name, I am important. Yet you wish to teach us that we become important only by becoming unimportant. It is by doing the little things out of true love and sacrifice that we become honored. This Lent, help me to find some way that I can serve others as Jesus did. Amen.

Thursday the Second Week

At the rich man's gate lay a beggar named Lazarus, who was covered with sores. (Luke 16:20)

This true account appeared in the *New York Times*. On a subway out of Times Square, two beggars appeared at opposite ends of the car. Almost simultaneously they started moving toward the center of the train, holding tin cups as they went. The older man was blind and wore a sandwich board covered with news stories of his attempts to get a seeing-eye dog. The other beggar was a double amputee. For some reason, the passengers were being unusually generous to the amputee. As they approached the center of the car, the amputee moved deftly aside and as they passed he took a coin from the cup in his lap and dropped it into the blind man's outstretched container, receiving the response, "Thank you, God bless you!"

Reflection
This Lent, practice the gift of almsgiving. There are many people who long for the scraps from our table. We may not consider ourselves well-off. Maybe we are even struggling to make ends meet, but we can give something, even if just a coin. There are no excuses.

Daily Prayer
Lord, too often I spend my time listing what I don't have rather than appreciating how much I already have. I allow my needs to be my excuse for not giving. Lord, help me to know that my possessions do not belong to me. Teach me to know that in giving I become wealthy. Father, let me understand that in helping those in need, I am helping your son, Jesus. Lord, fill me with a generous heart. Amen.

Friday the Second Week

When Joseph's brothers saw that their father loved him best of all his sons, they hated Joseph so much that they would not even greet him.
(Genesis 37:4)

The story is told of two shopkeepers who were bitter rivals. One night an angel appeared to one of the shopkeepers in a dream and said, "God has sent me to teach you a lesson. He will give you anything you ask for, but I want you to know that whatever you get, your competitor across the street will get twice as much.

"Would you like to be wealthy? You can be very wealthy, but he will be twice as rich. Do you want to live a long and healthy life? You can, but his life will be longer and happier. Ask for whatever you desire. But whatever you get he will get twice as much." The man frowned, thought for a moment and said, "All right. My request is that God strike me blind in one eye."

Reflection

Perhaps surprisingly, jealousy and envy don't hurt the other person nearly as much as they hurt the one who is jealous or envious. These feelings can destroy us. Too often they blind us to how much God has blessed us. The key in battling jealousy is to avoid making comparisons. We should accept our limitations but be mindful of our gifts. Today let us be aware of and grateful for all that God has given us.

Daily Prayer

Lord, help me to avoid the cancer of jealousy, because your peace cannot coexist with a jealous heart. Impress upon me how richly I have been blessed. May I thank and praise you not only for my gifts, but for the gifts you have bestowed on others as well. May my heart seek to please you, Lord, more than myself. Amen.

Saturday the Second Week

You will cast all our sins into the depths of the sea. (Micah 7:19)

Can you believe how many commercials are on during a football game??!! (Actually, sometimes the commercials are better than the game.) I have friends who watch the Super Bowl not for the game but to watch the commercials. My friend Tim, however, has no patience for the "down time." He watches an entire NFL game in less than an hour. He tapes the game and zips through the commercials, time-outs, and huddles. He is only interested in the "good stuff"—the action!

Reflection

When we die it will be the same way with God. The Lord will sit us down and we'll watch a video titled, *This Is Your Life*. We may squirm because we are afraid of what we might see, but this is a great video with a tremendously happy ending.

In watching our video, we'll notice that there are "blanks," and "blanks," and then more "blanks." In fact there are hundreds of blanks! These are all the times that God has forgiven us. Lent is the perfect time to begin erasing the mistakes in our life. Seek God's forgiveness. We simply have to ask and our sins are erased.

Daily Prayer

Dear Jesus, thank you so much for the priceless gift of forgiving our sins. You died so that we may live. Though this gift cost you your life it is granted to us so easily. All we need do is ask with a sincere heart. This Lent I want to turn away from sin and gain your pardon. Grant me the grace to seek forgiveness so that I may live in peace as your child. Amen.

Third Sunday of Lent

Remove the sandals from your feet for the place where you stand is holy ground. (Exodus 3:5)

In a certain parish, it was the practice in preparation for baptism to give instructions to the parents and sponsors. It was also the custom to invite relatives and friends to a buffet luncheon afterwards. Just before the ceremony the priest asked the father of the baby: "Baptism is a serious step. Are you prepared for it?"

"I think so," answered the father, "my wife has a couple of platters of finger food, plenty of cookies, and cakes."

"I don't mean that," injected the padre. "I mean, are you prepared spiritually?" "Oh, sure," exclaimed the father. "I've got a case of beer, a gallon of wine, and a case of whisky. Do you think that will be enough?"

Reflection

What place in our lives do we reserve for the sacred? What is holy in our lives? We are quite attentive to the things and matters of the world but often we neglect the sacred.

Our church is a holy place but it doesn't stop there. Families can be sacred, our home should be a safe shelter. Our very hearts are holy dwellings. Lent is a good time to recognize the hand and presence of God in the ordinary and mundane. God's presence makes everything holy and sacred.

Daily Prayer

Dear God, too many times I overlook your sacred presence. I restrict you to the church and leave you there. Open the eyes of my heart to see your presence in everyday occurrences. Lord, be present in my home, with my loved ones, and with me. I don't need to go great distances to find you. You are here and it is holy ground. Amen.

Monday the Third Week

Naaman…was highly esteemed and respected by the master, for through him the Lord had brought victory to Aram. But valiant as he was, the man was a leper. (2 Kings 5:1)

When the legendary salesman was asked his secrets of success, he gave a humble shrug. "I'm sure you all know the cardinal rules: know your product; make lots of calls; never take no for an answer. But honestly, I owe my success to consistently missing a three-foot putt by two inches whenever I play with my clients."

Reflection

Can I give you a bit of good news? You don't have to be perfect. In fact, we enjoy and appreciate people who make mistakes— then we don't look as bad. As great as Naaman was, he was a leper. He wasn't perfect. Maybe we are not lepers in the physical sense, but we all have our faults and weaknesses. Some of us just conceal them better. Imperfection is part of being human. We can begin to accept this fact by offering to the Lord not only our triumphs and successes, but our failures and disappointments. In God's hands, they can be turned into blessings.

Daily Prayer

Lord, I often don't want to acknowledge my failures and weaknesses. I try my best to hide them, disguise them, and even deny them. At times, I am even ashamed of my weakness. Though I may be able to fool others, I can't fool you. You know me through and through, just as I am. Help me, Lord, to accept myself as you accept me. May your grace transform me so that I may reflect your continual support and care. Amen.

Tuesday the Third Week

Lord, when others do me wrong, how often must I forgive them? Seven times? (Matthew 18:21)

When her late husband's will was read, a widow learned he had left the bulk of his fortune to another woman. Enraged, she rushed to change the inscription on her spouse's tombstone.

"Sorry, lady," said the stonecutter. "I inscribed 'Rest in Peace' on your order. I can't change it now."

"Very well," the widow said grimly. "Just add 'Until We Meet Again.'"

Reflection

No doubt it is difficult to forgive, especially if we are wronged gravely. That is why forgiveness is mentioned so often in the gospel. We are to forgive not only the trifles when it is easy, but even when the wound cuts deeply. "Not seven times but seventy times seven."

Are we carrying any grudges? How long will we hold on to them? Lent is a time of cleansing and letting go. If we can't forgive at this moment, we must pray for the gift to want to forgive. It is a step in the right direction.

Daily Prayer

Dear God, it is difficult to forgive and yet I know I must. I wish it were easier. I have been wronged, hurt, and mistreated, and sometimes I don't want to forgive. It just doesn't seem fair. When I believe and act this way, open my eyes to see that I am only hurting myself. You have forgiven me so much and as your disciple I must do the same. Lord, help me in those difficult moments. Amen.

Wednesday the Third Week

Take care and be earnestly on your guard not to forget the things which your own eyes have seen, nor let them slip from your memory as long as you live, but teach them to your children and to your children's children. (Deuteronomy 4:9)

During one of the natural disasters that hit California, residents had to evacuate their homes immediately. They looked about at all the things they had collected and loved and cared for for so many years: works of art, furniture, mementoes. There was no time to take any of them. A lifetime of accumulated possessions had to be left behind. There was only time to gather what they could carry in their arms.

It is interesting to hear what people took as they escaped. One woman took her grocery discount coupons, a man his box of tools. Some took family albums, kitchen utensils, letters, and even a television. Another took his daughter's favorite toys—the teddy bear she couldn't sleep without and her Cabbage Patch doll.

Reflection

What would you carry? What do you value and treasure? As the Israelites fled from Egypt, Moses reminded them that they must make sure to preserve and hand down their faith. This they could not do without. Of all things we wish to give to our young, where do we place our faith? In our efforts to give them the best, let us offer them the greatest gift, our faith and trust in Jesus.

Daily Prayer

Dear Lord, in our desire to give our loved ones the best, we sometimes overlook the most important treasure, that is, knowledge of you. May I give this gift to others not only by my words but through my actions and witness. If I succeed in giving this precious gift, I know I have given the very best. Amen.

Thursday the Third Week

Say to them: This is the nation which does not listen to the voice of the Lord its God, or take correction. (Jeremiah 7:28)

A woman whose hobby was gardening had to go out of town for a few days, leaving her husband in charge of her plants. After giving him detailed instructions, the woman pleaded, "And please talk to them occasionally."

"I'd feel like a fool," said her husband, who was not so avid about greenery.

When she returned, she found everything to be just fine. "You did a good job, dear," she said. "Did you talk to the plants?"

"No, I didn't," he replied. "I read the paper out loud in the morning and evening and if they wanted to listen it was up to them."

Reflection

Jeremiah speaks of the nation Israel turning a deaf ear to God. In many ways that can be said of our nation. God speaks to us, but we often choose not to listen. Rather than blaming the nation, however, we must realize that listening begins with each individual. It begins with each one of us. Do we listen to God's voice, God's prompting, God's nudges? Have we chosen to ignore God's voice and be about our own business? Despite what others may do, we need to heed and obey the Word of the Lord. Today is a great day to listen.

Daily Prayer

Lord, touch my ears. Better yet, touch my heart, and remove my deafness. Often I hear your voice but I'd rather not listen. Help me not to be foolish. Each day may I be humble enough to listen to your voice. Speak Lord, for I am listening. Amen.

Friday the Third Week

You shall love the Lord your God with all your heart, with all your soul, with all your mind, and with all your strength. (Mark 12:30)

For weeks, the couple had gone from showroom to showroom as the husband scrutinized new cars. Even after inspecting all of the cars carefully, he couldn't make up his mind.

"My, how you've changed," his wife chided him. "You married me three weeks after you saw me."

"Listen," he replied impatiently, "buying a car is serious business!"

Reflection

Getting to heaven is also serious business. Often we let many other cares and concerns cloud our view on what is of utmost importance. We become so wrapped up in the cares of the world that we overlook what is most important: our eternal salvation.

Jesus teaches us that we must love God above all things and that God must be first in our life. What is important to us? What is first in our lives? If Jesus isn't at the top of the list, we may have our priorities confused. During this time of conversion, let us give Jesus first place in our hearts.

Daily Prayer

Father, your son Jesus reminds us that we must love you above all things. I know this but I often fail to put it into practice. I just get so caught up in getting through everyday life. Dear God, though I may not always show it, I want to love you above all things. Help me to put this into practice. Amen.

Saturday the Third Week

"O God, be merciful to me, a sinner." ...This man went home from the temple justified. (Luke 18:13–14)

When John Lambert was called for jury duty in a drug trial in New York, he was most willing to serve but was disqualified. It was discovered that he happened to be the defendant in that case.

"I was prepared to find myself not guilty," he professed.

(From *One Minute Meditations for Busy People*, ©1996 by Rev. John Hampsch, C.M.F. Published by Servant Publications, Box 8617, Ann Arbor, MI 48107. Used with permission.)

Reflection

The first step in forgiveness is recognizing and admitting one's sinfulness. In the parable that Jesus tells in today's gospel, it is the tax collector who admits his sinfulness and is forgiven, not the self-righteous Pharisee. How often do we feel the need to be forgiven? Can we recognize and admit our weaknesses? Only by first admitting our sinfulness can we grow in God's grace. Offer today that simple prayer, "O God, be merciful to me, a sinner."

Daily Prayer

Lord, I come before you with no excuses or alibis. I'm not going to blame anyone or anything. I want to be straightforward and honest. I have sinned. I have failed to do right, and I have chosen to do wrong. I am sorry and ask your forgiveness. Please help me to say sincerely the prayer of the tax collector, "Be merciful to me, a sinner." This is who I am. Amen.

Fourth Sunday of Lent

This brother of yours was dead, and has come back to life. He was lost and is found. (Luke 15:32)

⌘

As a young boy one of my favorite book series was "Curious George." Surely you must remember the mischievous antics of that lovable monkey. He was always getting into trouble, whether flying a kite, swimming, or riding a bicycle. Once he almost landed in prison!

Just as certain that George would end up in danger, the Man in the Yellow Hat always came to the rescue. No matter how much trouble George got into, the Man in the Yellow Hat would always love him.

Reflection

God is like the Man in the Yellow Hat. That's a beautiful message, not only for children but for all of us. No matter how often we fail or sin, God is never going to stop loving us. This is what Jesus tells us over and over again in Scripture. Although we stray from the path of what is right and good, God waits for us always with open arms. Rejoice: God's love has found us!

Daily Prayer

Dear Father, I am that prodigal son, that prodigal daughter. I have been given so much and I have wasted it. I have run away from you. I, too, feel ashamed and unworthy. Help me now to stop focusing on myself and to walk with you. May I feel the joy and happiness of knowing that you love me. Lord, I can celebrate and rejoice because I belong to you. Amen.

Monday the Fourth Week

For I create Jerusalem to be a joy and its people to be a delight.
(Isaiah 65:18)

❧❧❧

There is a story about Groucho Marx and a priest. It seems that the priest was walking along a busy boulevard in Los Angeles when he recognized the great comedian. He tentatively approached him: "Pardon me, but aren't you Groucho Marx?" "Yes, I am, Father," the comedian replied, raising and lowering his eyebrows while tipping his cigar in his trademark fashion. "Well," said the priest, "I just want to thank you for all the joy and laughter you have brought into this world." The comedian is said to have replied, "And I would like to thank you, Father, for all the joy and laughter you have taken out of this world."

Reflection

Too often, we Christians are accused of being too somber, overly serious, and focused only on our trials and sufferings. In reality we should be the most joyful people in the world regardless of our problems and burdens. We know Jesus! Knowing him is far greater than any problem or hardship. Do we experience this joy in the Lord? Do we bring this joy to others? During this season of Lent, let us be a people of joy and hope, for Christ lives in us.

Daily Prayer

Lord, you have blessed us with your Spirit, your sign of joy and peace. Too often I fail to acknowledge these gifts and allow the trials of life to quench my happiness. Fill me again with your Spirit so that I may share in and reflect your presence in my life. Amen.

Tuesday the Fourth Week

When Jesus saw the sick man lying there, he said to him, "Do you want to be healed?" (John 5:6)

A woman explained to the psychiatrist that her husband thought he was the Lone Ranger. "How long has this been going on?" asked the doctor.

"About fifteen years."

"Bring him in, and I'll cure him."

The woman nodded. "That's the right thing to do," she conceded, then hesitated: "But Tonto is so good with the children."

Reflection

What a strange question for Jesus to ask a man who had been sick for thirty-eight years! Who wouldn't want to be healed? Yet there is a catch. Wholeness means taking on responsibility and enacting change in our life-style, and change is never easy.

Do we want to be healed—be it physically, emotionally, or spiritually? Are we willing to expend the energy, time, and sacrifice it may demand? Perhaps we like where we are; we're comfortable and may not want to undertake the work it requires to change. If we accept following Jesus radically, it may disrupt our life. Are we ready for this?

Daily Prayer

Gracious God, so often I pray for your help. I hope and expect you to work wonders in my life, and when you don't, I am disappointed. Father, help me realize that I can be healed if I open myself to your transforming grace. If I accept your son, Jesus, if I am willing to carry my cross, I can be healed. I can be reborn. Help me, Father, to say "yes" to you and to your son Jesus. Amen.

Wednesday the Fourth Week

Can a mother forget her infant, be without tenderness for the child of her womb? Even should she forget, I will never forget you.

(Isaiah 49:15)

An elderly man was sitting on a park bench in tears. A police officer came up and asked him what was wrong. "I'm seventy-five years old," sobbed the man. "I have a twenty-five-year-old wife at home who is beautiful, charming, and madly in love with me."

"So what's the problem?"

"I can't remember where I live!"

Reflection

Isaiah's words in today's first reading are a tremendous consolation. No matter how complex the world may be, no matter how small and insignificant we may feel, we are important to God. God is concerned about us, our desires, our hopes, our fears, our worries and problems. Others may not notice but God cares, for we are precious in God's sight. No matter what happens, no matter how greatly we may fail, God will never forget us: we are assured of that. In moments of doubt and even despair, remember God's eternal love.

Daily Prayer

Loving God, so often I feel small and insignificant. I wonder if I really matter. With the billions of people on the planet, do you know and care about me? Am I important to you? Maybe my problems are not that significant compared to all the world's difficulties, but they matter to me. Do they matter to you? You tell me they do. Lord, in these moments of doubt, reassure me of your immense love for me. Amen.

Thursday the Fourth Week

You do not have God's word abiding in your hearts. (John 5:38)

The Bible has served many purposes. Some use it for a paperweight, family album, or to hide documents. I heard of a fellow who choked to death in his attempt to swallow one. It wasn't that he was hungry, but he figured it would purge him of sin. Now that's a hard pill to swallow!

Reflection

Does God's Word abide in our hearts? This can't be accomplished by actually eating the sacred book, but by quiet prayer and reflective reading. Setting aside a few minutes even on a busy day to ponder Scripture helps plant God's peace in our hearts.

Here's some advice that I was given years ago. Place your Bible on your pillow so that before going to sleep you have to remove it. Then read just one line each evening: that's all it takes, one line. It may not seem like much but in time we will grow in knowledge. Perhaps this Lent we can begin the healthy practice of *reading*, not *eating*, God's Word.

Daily Prayer

Dear God, I often hear and sense your promptings to spend more time with you. I want to, but I don't. It just seems too hard to find the time and solitude. Help me to realize that it is better to do a little than to do nothing at all. Lord, may I set a few moments aside to be with you for I know you are waiting for me. Today, Lord, let me spend just a moment with you. Amen.

Friday the Fourth Week

Many are the afflictions of the righteous, but the Lord rescues them from them all. (Psalm 34:19)

Former UCLA football coach Pepper Rodgers, after a disastrous season, stated: "I had only one friend—my dog. Even my wife was mad at me! I told her a man ought to have at least two friends. She agreed, and bought me another dog."

Reflection

Often when we are hurting, in pain, or down on our luck, we feel most alone. It seems that nobody cares, not even those from whom we expect it. We may not even want to be with others. We may want to be left alone. It is in those moments when life appears most bleak that God can reach us.

Jesus knew pain, desertion, and humiliation. God not only knew, God cared. In your prayer time, offer to the Lord your troubles, concerns, and tribulations. Allow God to comfort you and experience his abiding presence. Trust that God is there!

Daily Prayer

God, all too often when I am hurt, angry, or discouraged, I push away those who care the most. I stubbornly refuse their help. I push you aside as well. Maybe I think that you can't be bothered with my problems.

Today I am reminded that it is at those moments that you are closest to me. In my pain, may I trust and confide in you? Heal my brokenness, O Lord. Amen.

Saturday the Fourth Week

O Lord, my God, in you I take refuge. (Psalm 7:1)

On his last day at work before a layoff, a Los Angeles man received an emergency call to hurry home, where he was horrified to find his house in ashes and his wife and four small children dead. Totally bereft of family, house, job, and even insurance, he wept in his neighbor's arms, "I have nothing left now but God."

(From *One-Minute Meditations for Busy People,* copyright by Rev. John Hampsch, C.M.F. Published by Servant Publications, Box 8617, Ann Arbor, MI 48107. Used with permission.)

Reflection

Can you imagine such a tragedy? How would we react if we lost everything? It is beyond comprehension. At moments such as this, however, our faith is truly tested. Either we deepen our faith or abandon it.

In our tragedies, we can experience God in a whole different realm. When God is all we have, then we realize how much God means to us.

Daily Prayer

Lord Jesus, you came to show us the way. You promised never to leave us orphaned but to remain with us. How wonderful you are! Lord Jesus, in times of loss and heartache, may I turn and trust in you. For you are all I have or will ever need, you are my refuge. Amen.

Fifth Sunday of Lent

I have accounted all else rubbish so that Christ may be my wealth and I may be in him. (Philippians 3:8)

Before the Soviet Union was finally opened up in the early 1990s, Christians were persecuted. Luta Kosachevich, a Christian, was arrested for printing Bibles.

At her trial she testified: "I love life, I love the blue sky. I love the budding trees and flowers but more than anything else I love God and I'll give my life to serve him." Having lost everything in prison, including her health, she wrote, "It's worth it to believe!"

Reflection

Such faith, such love for God! How does one experience what Luta and St. Paul did, who felt that nothing else mattered except knowing Jesus? Many of us know Jesus but are still strongly attached to the things of this world. Sometimes they control us.

Lent is a time to prioritize our life. Don't allow yourself to get caught up in the rat race. Take time to pray, even if for a few moments. Put God first!

Daily Prayer

Dear God, I want to be on fire. I want to be consumed by the love of Jesus. I want to belong totally to him. Yet I cling to the world. I want nice clothes, a comfortable house, and the best car. Little by little let me detach myself from the things of this world and become more attached to your son, Jesus. May Jesus always be first in my heart. Amen.

Monday the Fifth Week

Let the one among you who has no sin be the first to cast a stone at her. (John 8:7)

Behind the checkout case register, the clerk watched a portly fellow place his beer, wine, cigars, and an "adult" book on the counter. As she rang up these items, he suddenly dropped a candy bar in front of her.

"Oops, I almost forgot," he said guiltily. "My one vice."

Reflection

We all have faults; some of us are just better in hiding them or even denying them. Once we recognize and acknowledge our own weaknesses, we can more easily accept weakness in someone else. Christ asks us not to judge in condemnation, for if that were the standard we would all be condemned.

Lord, help us not to judge and condemn through our speech or thoughts, but rather to see ourselves as we really are—forgiven of our faults and in need of your constant mercy.

Daily Prayer

Father, you sent your son, Jesus, not to condemn the world but to save it. If you, who are all good, can accept me in my sinfulness, then help me to do the same. Help me realize that we all have failed and it is only through love and not condemnation that we can change. Amen.

Tuesday the Fifth Week

Make a saraph (serpent) and mount it on a pole, and if anyone who has been bitten looks at it, that person will recover. (Numbers 21:8)

Alexander Solzhenitsyn tells of a time in the Siberian prison when he was weary from hard labor, weak from a starvation diet, and in pain from an untreated illness. He was being forced to shovel sand hour after backbreaking hour. Finally he felt he could not go on. He just stopped, knowing that the guards would beat him severely, perhaps even to death.

Just then another prisoner, a fellow Christian, took his shovel handle and, right at Solzhenitsyn's feet, he drew in the sand the sign of the cross. Then he quickly erased it. But when Solzhenitsyn caught the glimpse of the cross, all hope and courage of the Gospel flooded his soul and enabled him to hold on. He said that he was saved that day by the sign of the cross.

Reflection

The cross is our sign of life, hope, and faith. As the Israelites wandered through the desert, God told Moses to mount an image of a saraph so that those bitten by serpents would live, and so it happened.

When we are bitten by the poison of sin, discouragement, and despair, may we look at the cross and be reminded of God's great love and care. May this sign of God's great gift to us renew and strengthen us in our resolve.

Daily Prayer

Father, thank you for your son, Jesus, who obediently gave his life for us on the cross. When I feel downtrodden, hopeless, and without life, may I look to the cross. May that reminder of your great love renew and strengthen me. I know that with the cross before me, I can go on. Amen.

Wednesday the Fifth Week

We will not serve your god or worship the golden statue which you set up. (Daniel 3:18)

One prominent psychiatrist has called our preoccupation with money the number one crippling disease in this country. He credits our "money sickness" as the source of much frustration and anxiety.

The love of money can cripple us, diminish us, and even destroy us more effectively than any other form of illness. It can cause physical illness, demolish marriages, break up families, and even drive some to murder and suicide. Doctors now tell us that often they are able to trace internal medical problems directly to patients' attitudes toward money and possessions—the *economic* aspects of their lives.

As the man said to his psychiatrist: "By the time I discovered that money doesn't buy happiness, I had already earned five million dollars."

Reflection

As much as we may believe that our false idols—whether money, prestige, or body image—do not buy us happiness, we still fall into the fallacy of chasing after them. We are convinced that if we possess the things that we desire, we will be satisfied. Yet it doesn't work that way. Only God can make a person happy. Seek the Lord with your whole heart and you will not be disappointed.

Daily Prayer

Lord, I am often fooled by the commercialism of life. I somehow believe that my life is incomplete without the wealth and comforts that call seductively to me. Help me to realize that they are false gods offering false hopes. Only by loving you and living in your Spirit can I find true joy. May my heart seek only what you desire. May my heart desire you alone. Amen.

Thursday the Fifth Week

God said to Abraham: "On your part, you and your descendants after you must keep my covenant throughout the ages."

(Genesis 17:9)

❧❧❧❧❧

Little Johnny was thrilled at his first day of kindergarten. "It was great," he told his delighted parents when he came home. So they naturally figured they'd have no trouble getting him up and out for kindergarten in the mornings to come—much to their relief. But when the second morning arrived, Johnny was reluctant to roll out of bed and get dressed. And at breakfast he complained about having to go to kindergarten.

"I thought you liked school," his father commented.

"Oh, I did like it the first time," Johnny replied. "but if I'd known it was every day I'd never have signed on."

Reflection

The challenge in keeping God's covenant is that it is not for a day, a week, or a year, but for a lifetime. Remaining faithful to God is not just for the elderly, or the religious, or just during Lent. It is for everybody all the time. Sometimes it is not easy, but all God asks of us is to take one day at a time and follow his command. God on his part promises to support and strengthen us when we are tempted to give up the fight. Just take one day at a time.

Daily Prayer

Dear God, there is no vacation or time off in following your commands. Every day I have the choice of saying "yes" to you. Yet it isn't always that easy. I am tempted and easily swayed. I know what I should do but I don't always do it. Lord, during this Lent, purify my intentions and help me in my resolve to obey your commands. Amen.

Friday the Fifth Week

Sing to the Lord, praise the Lord who has rescued the life of the poor from the power of the wicked. (Jeremiah 20:13)

"One time when my children were toddlers," the woman said, "the phone rang and my oldest picked it up. 'Hi, Daddy,' she said and began telling her father about her day. She then passed the phone to her brother and sister as was the custom whenever my husband called from work.

"When it was my turn to talk I took the receiver and said, 'Hi, hon.'

"'Thank God, lady,' the voice on the other end replied. 'I just called to tell you that the wallpaper you ordered is here!'"

Reflection

We need to be like those little children, excited, jubilant, and overjoyed in speaking to their father (at least they thought it was their dad!). We should feel likewise when we speak to our heavenly Father. God loves us, rescues us from death, and continues to lead us forth.

Unfortunately we don't always feel like being loved, rescued, or led forth. Perhaps we take too much for granted or focus on only what is lacking in our lives. But we are blessed; we truly are. So yes, sing to the Lord, praise God who is so good!

Daily Prayer

Heavenly Father, touch my heart. May I feel the excitement and joy that shines in one who is in love with God. I want to be alive and on fire for you. I have much to praise and thank you for. You are my Father and I am your child. Nothing can mean more than this. Bless my tongue so I may sing your praises. Amen.

Saturday the Fifth Week

They shall be my people, and I will be their God. (Ezekiel 37:23)

There is the story of a man who was very unhappy to be discharged by his psychiatrist after years of analysis. "You're cured," said the doctor.

"Some cure!" the man snorted. "When I came here I was Napoleon Bonaparte. Now I'm nobody!"

Reflection

The Lord Jesus came to cure us. He cured not only those afflicted with physical ailments, but spiritual as well. Jesus came to remove our illusions, our pretenses, and our masks. We are somebody not because of the clothes we wear, the car we drive, or the home we live in. We are special because we are loved by God. We are made in God's image and likeness.

Despite the pressure and influence from the world to conform, we don't have to give in. We don't need to be the best, the most popular, or the most successful. All we have to be is the person God has created, unique and loved by our creator.

Daily Prayer

Dear God, I am quite mindful of what I lack, need, and desire. I am often reminded of my shortcomings and failings. I attempt to overcome them by my possessions, friends, and approval from others. I overlook your love for me. I dismiss the fact that I am your child, as if it didn't matter! Allow me to recall at those moments of self-deprecation, my greatest gift: I belong to you. May that be enough for me. Amen.

Passion (or Palm) Sunday

Blessed be he who comes as king in the name of the Lord.

(Luke 19:38)

Rose Kennedy would always explain the Catholic faith to her children, especially on big feasts. After one Easter story concerning Jesus' entrance into Jerusalem on a donkey, the crucifixion, entombment, and resurrection, little Jack asked, "Mother, we know what happened to Jesus Christ, but what happened to the donkey?"

Reflection

This Sunday marks the beginning of the most sacred week of the year for all Christendom—Holy Week. We may know the facts of the story, the trial, and the suffering of Jesus. But it doesn't mean we know the heart of the story. Part of the problem may be that we know the account too well and it remains simply a pious story from the past.

This week we can bring it alive and make it mean something. No matter how we may have spent these last five weeks, we can still make this last week truly special. Pray, read the Scriptures, and ask to know the story not only in your head but in your heart.

Daily Prayer

Loving God, how often I get caught up in my day-to-day concerns and forget about you. Now, O Lord, I begin Holy Week and I don't want this week to pass me by. Help me, Lord, with your promptings and nudges to spend time in prayer and quiet reflection. It is Holy Week, Lord, and I want to be holy: I want to please you. May this week be a blessing in your sight. Amen.

Monday of Holy Week

I formed you and set you as a covenant of the people, a light for the nations. (Isaiah 42:6)

There was an elderly woman who stood on a street corner, hesitant to cross because there was no traffic signal to control the heavy flow of cars and trucks. As she waited, a gentleman came up beside her and asked, "May I cross over with you?" Relieved, she thanked him and took his arm.

The path they took was anything but safe. The man seemed to be confused as they dodged traffic and walked in a zig-zag pattern across the street. "You almost got us killed!" the woman exclaimed in anger when they finally reached the curb. "You walk like you're blind." "I am," he replied. "That's why I asked if I could cross with you."

Reflection

As Christians we are not to walk alone. Our faith isn't about Jesus and me, but rather, Jesus and us. God has given each of us talents, gifts, and abilities not only for our satisfaction and enjoyment but to reveal God's care and presence to others. We are to be God's light to those living in darkness, to those who do not know Christ. They are the ones we need to walk with. Let us walk together with our God who supports us in our struggles. Most of all, let us never walk alone.

Daily Prayer

God, my Father, I am your child but I am not an only child. Each person is my brother or sister and is loved by you. I cannot hope to please you by only focusing on my own needs and desires, no matter how important they may be. To walk with you I must walk with others. Be with me, Lord, so that I may be with others even in those moments when I'd rather not bother. Amen.

Tuesday of Holy Week

The Lord called me from birth, from my mother's womb he gave me my name. (Isaiah 49:1)

❧

I saw this article titled "Look Who's Walking" in People magazine:

"At birth Madeline weighed all of 9.9 *ounces*. As Dr. Jonathan Maraskas held her in the palm of his hand, she began squirming and let out a little mew. 'She looked at me with her eyes open,' Maraskas says, 'and I could not ignore her.' Today, Madeline is a spunky kid who shouts 'out' when she wants to be sprung from her crib. Fortunately, her mental development is normal, but she will be on the small side as an adult. That's not too bad for a child who wasn't expected to make it."

Reflection

One of the great horrors of our nation is the atrocity of abortion, the destroying of an innocent life. Isaiah tells us that God has formed us and knows us in our mother's womb. Even before our birth God had a plan for us. Abortion destroys God's design. It is an abomination that cries out to the God of justice.

Lent is a time of penance, a time to seek forgiveness and change our ways. During this season, we can pray and offer sacrifice that the destroying of innocent life will not continue to plague our nation.

Daily Prayer

Father, you are the creator of all life. It is not for us to decide who should live or die. In your eyes, all life is precious, from the very young to the very old. Enkindle in us, O Lord, the deep reverence and respect for this most precious gift of life, for without it nothing is sacred, nothing is valued. Amen.

Wednesday of Holy Week

The Lord God has given me a well-trained tongue, that I might know how to speak to the weary a word that will rouse them. (Isaiah 50:4)

Three Vietnamese women were openly speaking of Jesus. They were put in jail, but undaunted, they began spreading the news of Jesus to their cellmates.

The guards were commanded to beat them, but they were touched by the Holy Spirit and could not strike them. They were brought before the chief. "Get them out of here," he ordered. "No, we have more work to do," the ladies replied.

To be sent out of prison they had to sign a confession. Eventually they agreed to leave but they wouldn't admit to any fault. Finally they gave in to signing an accusation which read, "Loving God more than normal."

Reflection

There is a power in faith, a faith that is not afraid, ashamed, or fearful, a faith that is willing to witness, to act, and to shine. That is true strength and conviction. If we know and love God's Word, we can speak to the weary, the angry, the hurt. Let us ask God to use us, praise God for using us, and finally, love God more than normal!

Daily Prayer

God, often I feel so discouraged. It seems that the world has gone mad. I wonder if anybody believes in you. I feel alone and overwhelmed. Yet you have sent me to be the light to others—to speak an encouraging word, to uplift, and to be a comfort. I admit that at times I am afraid and doubtful. It is in those times, Lord, that I need to trust in you. Help me, Lord, to be your witness. Amen.

Holy Thursday

As Jesus approached Simon Peter, Peter asked, "Lord, are you going to wash my feet?" (John 13:6)

While on a pilgrimage, Sister Maurice shared with me this story. The day before Holy Thursday, she told her class that they might see something on that night that they had never seen before in the sanctuary: "You might see twelve people getting their feet washed by the priest."

A little boy asked, "Why are they coming to church to have their feet washed? Aren't they big enough to wash their own feet?"

His friend retorted, "Boy, you don't know what you're talking about. They may be too fat to bend over and wash their own feet!"

Reflection

The fact is we are all unable to wash our own feet. We need Jesus to cleanse us. The Lord today not only cleanses the mere exterior, but he purifies our hearts from sin. We may not be one of the symbolic twelve to have our feet washed, but we can ask Jesus to cleanse and purify our hearts from sin.

Daily Prayer

Heavenly Father, today your son, Jesus, gives us his body and blood. How fortunate I am to be able to receive this most precious gift, for his body and blood cleanse me from sin. Wash me, Jesus, not just my feet or hands, but wash me entirely so that I may be born again in you. Each time I receive your body and blood, grant me the thirst to have my heart cleansed of the desire to do wrong. Amen.

Good Friday

He was wounded for our transgressions, crushed for our sins. By his bruises we are healed. (Isaiah 53:5)

There are many customs and traditions on Good Friday. Perhaps none are as excruciating as those followed in the Philippines. It is not unusual to have devout Christians commit themselves to a crucifixion. They permit themselves to be nailed to a cross. Those who are less courageous parade through the streets whipping their backs with bamboo sticks, bloodied and scarred for life. They do all this in the hope of gaining God's favor and imitating Christ in his suffering.

Reflection
We imitate Christ not by beating ourselves or punishing our bodies, but by our concern for the poor, the outcast, the alien. We share in his suffering when we feel the pain of the homeless, the hungry, and the downtrodden. That is how Christ wishes us to imitate him, not by crucifying ourselves. "Whatever you do for the least of my people you do for me."

Daily Prayer
O Lord Jesus, today we stop and reflect on how much you have given us. You suffered and died so that we may live. Lord, I run away from pain and suffering and do my best to avoid it. I want to be comfortable. Yet, as your disciple I can't be comfortable while so many are uncomfortable and suffering. Help me to help others. Then truly I can call myself your follower. Amen.

Holy Saturday

Because of the Jewish preparation day, they laid Jesus there, for the tomb was close at hand. (John 19:42)

A pompous CEO was addressing his employees and trying hard to impress them with his importance, especially with his importance in their working lives. "If I die tonight," he asked, "where would you be?"

One of the more outspoken employees said, "The question, sir, is if you died tonight, where would *you* be?"

Reflection

This is a good question, for all of us. As we approach the glorious feast of the Resurrection of our Lord, we can take time to ponder this monumental question—"If I were to die today, where would I be?" If we believe in Jesus as our Lord and have followed him, the answer is HEAVEN!

Daily Prayer

Loving God, there is a stillness, a quietness in the air. Holy Thursday and Good Friday have passed, and now we wait to celebrate Easter Sunday. Easter is here but not quite yet. In some way our life is similar. We want heaven but are not quite ready yet. Help me, Lord, to never lost sight of this ultimate goal. Each day may I be a step closer to heaven and to you. Amen.

XXIII TWENTY-THIRD PUBLICATIONS
P.O. Box 180 • Mystic, CT 06355 • 1-800-321-0411

9 780896 228924